Teddy Van Gough

DIRECTING YOUR DREAMS:

A Practical Guide to Filmmaking

Copyright © 2025 Praenova Solutions LLC. All rights reserved.

Directing Your Dreams is a work dedicated to empowering filmmakers with the knowledge and strategies needed to navigate the film industry successfully. This book provides insights into storytelling, production, marketing, and business strategies, equipping readers with essential tools to bring their visions to life.

No part of this book may be reproduced, stored in a retrieval system, or transmitted in any form or by any means—electronic, mechanical, photocopying, recording, or otherwise—without express written permission from the publisher, except for brief quotations used in reviews or academic discussions.

ISBN-13: 979-8-9925094-1-0

Cover design by: Praenova Solutions LLC Printed in the United States of America

Chapter 1: **9**
    Development - From Idea to Script...................... 9
    Finding Inspiration.. 9
    Structuring Your Story... 10
    Building a Solid Foundation................................ 12
    Writing the First Draft... 12
    Screenplay Formatting Essentials....................... 13
    Refining Your Script.. 14
    Preparing Your Script for Production................ 15

Chapter 2: **16**
    Pre-Production - Laying the Foundation........... 16
    Budgeting Basics.. 16
        Budget Allocation.. 16
        Below-the-Line Costs.................................. 18
        Additional Costs.. 18
    Case Study: The Blair Witch Project.................. 18
    Assembling Your Crew.. 19
        Key Positions to Fill..................................... 19
        Hiring the Right Team................................ 19
        Fostering Collaboration.............................. 20
        Crew Management Tips............................... 20

Chapter 3: **21**
    Directing - The Art of Bringing Your Vision to Life. 21
        Understanding the Director's Role.............. 21
        The Difference Between Blocking and Staging 21
        Blocking Techniques for Visual Storytelling.... 22

Staging for Emotional Impact......................23
Directing Actors: Communication Techniques... 23
Pulling the Best Performance.................... 24
Working with the Director of Photography. 24
On-Set Problem-Solving............................. 25

Chapter 4:..**26**
Shotlisting - A Crucial Tool for Filmmakers....... 26
Why Shotlisting Matters............................. 26
Creating an Effective Shot List......................27
Elements to Include................................... 27
Benefits of Shotlisting................................28

Chapter 5:..**29**
Production - Turning Plans into Reality............29
Running an Efficient Set.............................29
Key Departments and Their Functions....... 29
Maintaining a Productive Atmosphere....... 30
Shooting for the Edit................................. 31
Handling Unforeseen Challenges............... 32

Chapter 6:..**33**
Post-Production - Piecing It All Together.......... 33
The Editing Process....................................33
Collaborating with an Editor...................... 34
Sound Design and Foley Art....................... 34
Color Grading and Visual Effects................35
Music Scoring and Licensing...................... 35
Preparing Deliverables for Distribution...... 36

Chapter 7:..**38**
Chain of Title - Own it................................... 38

Key Components of Chain of Title Documents 38

The Importance of a Clean Chain of Title... 40

Best Practices for Managing Chain of Title.. 41

Chapter 8: **43**

Distribution and Marketing Strategies............... 43

Identifying Your Audience............................ 43

The Festival Circuit...................................... 44

Online Platforms and Streaming Services... 44

Traditional vs. Self-Distribution................... 45

Crafting a Marketing Strategy...................... 46

The Importance of Networking.....................47

Chapter 9: **49**

Understanding Your Target Audience............... 49

Research Your Genre and Subgenres................. 49

Analyze Competitors.. 49

Define Audience Demographics......................... 50

Develop Audience Personas................................50

Conduct Market Research.................................. 51

Test Your Assumptions.......................................51

Creating a minimum viable product (MVP),......51

such as a teaser or short preview, allows you to validate audience interest. Share this content with a selected group of viewers to gather feedback and fine-tune your approach............. 52

Explore Psychographics..................................... 52

Analyze Media Consumption Habits................. 52

Chapter 10: **54**

Attracting Investors and Financing Your Film... 54

    Developing a Compelling Pitch..................54
    Creating a Business Plan for Your Film........55
    Finding and Approaching Investors............56
    Crowdfunding Strategies..............................57
    Government Grants and Tax Incentives.......59
    Pitch Deck..60

Resources...62
    Professional Script Format Templates.............62
    Budgeting Spreadsheet Templates...................63
    Production Schedule Template........................64
    Call Sheet Template.......................................65
    Shot List Template..66

Overcoming Challenges and Staying Inspired..69
    Dealing with Creative Blocks............................69
    Managing Stress on Set...................................70
    Learning from Failure....................................71
    Staying Passionate About Your Craft................73

Epilogue..75
    Your Next Steps in Filmmaking.......................75
    Recommended Resources to Expand Your Knowledge..76
    Final Thoughts...77

Screenwriter's Workbook: Character Development Exercise..82
THE DIRECTOR'S NOTEBOOK........................89

Preface

Filmmaking is more than just an art form; it is a journey of vision, strategy, and execution. It is the synthesis of storytelling, technical prowess, and business acumen—a delicate balance between creative expression and structured discipline. Directing Your Dreams is a culmination of my journey, experiences, and insights, crafted to serve as a guiding tool for filmmakers at any stage of their career. Whether you are an aspiring director, an independent filmmaker, or an industry professional looking to refine your craft, this book is designed to help sharpen your knowledge and elevate your approach to filmmaking.

Over the last 15 years, I have developed an extensive skill set in corporate sales and management. These experiences have given me a deep understanding of branding, marketing, and the business strategies required to promote and monetize creative work. The ability to market a film effectively is just as important as producing one, and through my expertise in sales, I have cultivated strategies that will help filmmakers turn their passion projects into profitable and sustainable careers.

Beyond my corporate background, the last five years have been dedicated to immersing myself in the art and technical aspects of filmmaking. I have honed my skills in screenplay writing, directing, producing, and cinematography—allowing me to develop a holistic understanding of the filmmaking process. This hands-on experience has provided me with invaluable insights into both the creative and logistical challenges filmmakers face, and it has fueled my passion for sharing knowledge with others who are driven to succeed in this field.

The goal of Directing Your Dreams is simple: to provide filmmakers with a comprehensive tool they can use to achieve greatness in this industry. Through this book, I aim to bridge the gap between creativity and business, equipping readers with the mindset, strategies, and practical knowledge needed to navigate the evolving landscape of film. My hope is that this book not only serves as a resource but as a source of inspiration—encouraging filmmakers to take control of their careers, embrace their unique voices, and turn their dreams into reality.

Filmmaking is an ever-changing industry, one that rewards those who are willing to innovate, adapt, and persist. This book is a testament to the belief that with the right knowledge, strategy, and dedication, success is within reach for any filmmaker willing to put in the work.

Welcome to Directing Your Dreams: A Practical Guide to Filmmaking. Your journey to mastering the art, business, and impact of filmmaking starts here.

Chapter 1:

Development - From Idea to Script

Turning a spark of inspiration into a fully realized screenplay is both an art and a disciplined process. It takes passion, skill, and perseverance. This chapter will walk you through the fundamental steps of crafting your script, from discovering your inspiration to preparing it for production.

Finding Inspiration

Every great film begins with a compelling idea. Whether it's drawn from personal experiences, an eye-catching headline, or a random thought, shaping an idea into a solid concept is the first crucial step.

Start by asking yourself:

- What themes genuinely excite me?
- What message do I want my audience to take away?
- Who am I making this film for?

Here are some effective ways to ignite your creativity:

1. **Reflect on personal experiences** – Your life, emotions, and observations can add authenticity and depth to your story.
2. **Explore various media** – Dive into books, films, music, and art to find inspiration from different perspectives.
3. **Stay informed** – Current events and social issues can spark powerful and relevant stories.
4. **Engage with visual arts** – A single image can inspire an entire narrative.
5. **Observe everyday life** – Watching people in public spaces can offer rich character insights.
6. **Document your dreams** – Your subconscious can offer fascinating story ideas.

Structuring Your Story

Once you've honed in on your idea, structuring your story is the next step. A well-structured screenplay keeps your audience engaged. The classic three-act structure is widely used:

1. **Act One:** *Setup*

    - Introduce characters and the world.
    - Establish the main conflict.

- Present the inciting incident that sets the story in motion.

2. **Act Two:** *Confrontation*

    - Deepen character arcs and introduce subplots.
    - Add obstacles and challenges.
    - Build momentum leading to the climax.

3. **Act Three:** *Resolution*

    - Tie up loose ends and resolve conflicts.
    - Deliver a satisfying conclusion.
    - Leave the audience with a lasting impression.

Other narrative structures, such as the "*Hero's Journey*" or "*nonlinear storytelling*", can offer unique storytelling approaches. Choose the one that aligns with your vision.

Building a Solid Foundation

1. **Develop compelling characters** – Ensure they have distinct goals, motivations, and internal conflicts.
2. **Outline your plot** – Map out key story beats and major turning points.
3. **Craft a concise logline** – A one or two-sentence summary that captures the essence of your story.
4. **Expand into a treatment** – Develop your logline into a detailed synopsis of 2-5 pages.
5. **Create a scene-by-scene breakdown** – This ensures a logical flow and consistent pacing.

Writing the First Draft

With your structure in place, dive into writing your first draft. The goal here is progress, not perfection.

- Establish a consistent writing routine.
- Keep characters at the forefront of the story.
- Show, don't tell – use action and dialogue effectively.
- Follow industry-standard screenplay formatting.
- Write freely and refine later.

Screenplay Formatting Essentials

Proper formatting ensures your script looks professional. Follow these key guidelines:

- Use **Courier 12-point font**.
- Maintain **1.5-inch left margins, 1-inch right margins**.
- Format scene headings as: **INT./EXT. LOCATION - TIME**.
- Capitalize character names on first introduction.
- Center all dialogue.

Example:

```
Unset
INT. COFFEE SHOP - DAY

JOHN, mid-30s, nervously taps his
fingers on the table.

          SARAH (O.S.)
     John, are you okay?

He looks up, forcing a smile.
```

```
                    JOHN
            Yeah... just thinking.
```

Refining Your Script

After completing your first draft, it's time to refine it through revisions and feedback.

1. Step away for a while to gain a fresh perspective.
2. Review your work critically, focusing on structure and pacing.
3. Seek constructive feedback from peers or writing groups.
4. Address weaknesses in character development and plot.
5. Polish dialogue to ensure authenticity.
6. Revise and rewrite until your script is as strong as possible.

Preparing Your Script for Production

Before your screenplay moves into production, a script breakdown is essential. This process involves:

1. Reading the script multiple times to identify logistical elements.
2. Categorizing all necessary elements, such as characters, locations, and props.
3. Creating breakdown sheets that list essential scene details.
4. Using a color-coded system to track key components.
5. Identifying special requirements such as stunts or effects.
6. Estimating scene lengths to aid in scheduling and budgeting.

By following these steps, you'll transform your initial concept into a well-structured and production-ready screenplay. Remember, screenwriting is an iterative process, and with each draft, you refine and strengthen your story.

Chapter 2:

Pre-Production - Laying the Foundation

Pre-production is the backbone of your film. Thoughtful and strategic planning in this phase can save you valuable time, money, and unnecessary stress down the road. Let's dive into the critical elements of pre-production that will position your project for success.

Budgeting Basics

Crafting a thorough budget is a fundamental step in any film project. A well-structured budget ensures resources are allocated wisely and prevents unexpected financial hurdles. Here's a breakdown of the key components:

Budget Allocation

Industry standards suggest the following breakdown for feature films:

- **Above-the-Line Costs:** 30%
- **Below-the-Line Costs:** 45%
- **Additional Costs:** 25%

For example, if you're working with a $500,000 independent film budget, it might look like this:

Category	Amount	Percentage
Above-the-Line	$150,000	30%
Below-the-Line	$225,000	45%
Additional Costs	$125,000	25%
Total	**$500,000**	**100%**

Above-the-Line Costs

These include:

- Development expenses
- Director, producer, and lead cast salaries
- Scriptwriting and revisions

Below-the-Line Costs

These cover:

- Crew wages
- Equipment rentals
- Location fees
- Transportation
- Catering
- Post-production work

Additional Costs

Often overlooked but critical elements include:

- Legal fees
- Production insurance
- A contingency fund (usually 10% of the budget)

Case Study: *The Blair Witch Project*

A brilliant example of budget efficiency is *The Blair Witch Project*. With an initial budget of just $60,000, the film ended up grossing a staggering $248 million worldwide. The key factors behind its success:

- A minimalist production approach
- Creative marketing tactics

- Capitalizing on emerging digital platforms

Assembling Your Crew

Building the right team is essential to ensure a seamless production process. Here's how to do it effectively:

Key Positions to Fill

- **Director** - The visionary behind the film
- **Producer** - Oversees logistics and ensures the project stays on track
- **Cinematographer** - Captures the visual essence
- **Sound Recordist** - Ensures top-notch audio
- **Production Designer** - Crafts the visual style

Hiring the Right Team

- Define clear roles and expectations upfront
- Tap into your existing network for reliable talent
- Leverage platforms like ProductionHub or Mandy to find professionals
- Prioritize skillset, experience, and team synergy

Fostering Collaboration

Take inspiration from directors like *Robert Altman*, who thrived on collaboration:

- Encourage open dialogue and creative input
- Allow for organic scene development
- Build an environment where everyone feels valued

Crew Management Tips

- Clearly communicate your vision and objectives
- Create a positive work culture to boost morale
- Promote open discussions to address challenges proactively
- Utilize project management tools such as Trello or Monday.com to stay organized and maintain seamless communication

By focusing on these foundational aspects—budgeting and crew assembly—you'll set yourself up for a smooth and successful film production. Remember, thorough planning and attention to detail now will pay dividends when it's time to roll the cameras.

Chapter 3:

Directing - The Art of Bringing Your Vision to Life

Understanding the Director's Role

The director serves as the creative force behind a film, shaping its overall look, feel, and tone. Their responsibilities include:

- Interpreting the script and developing a clear concept for the film
- Communicating their vision to the entire production team
- Overseeing all creative elements throughout pre-production, production, and post-production

Why it matters: A well-defined directorial vision ensures a unified and compelling final product, guiding all creative choices throughout the filmmaking journey.

The Difference Between Blocking and Staging

Though often confused, blocking and staging serve distinct purposes in filmmaking:

- **Blocking**: The precise movement and positioning of actors within a scene
- **Staging:** The overall arrangement of all elements within the frame, including set design, props, and lighting

Why it's important: Distinguishing these concepts empowers directors to craft a more nuanced and visually engaging storytelling approach.

Blocking Techniques for Visual Storytelling

Strategic blocking enhances the narrative and emotional weight of a scene by:

- Positioning actors to reflect relationships and power dynamics
- Integrating meaningful props and set elements for interaction
- Using depth and layering to highlight key elements and add visual interest

Why it matters: Thoughtful blocking conveys character dynamics and emotions without relying on dialogue, making scenes more immersive and expressive.

Staging for Emotional Impact

Staging plays a crucial role in amplifying the emotional resonance of a scene through:

- Composition techniques such as the rule of thirds and symmetry
- Adjusting character proximity to reflect their emotional states
- Utilizing lighting and color to enhance mood and underscore emotions

Why it's crucial: Effective staging guides the audience's attention and strengthens the film's emotional storytelling.

Directing Actors: Communication Techniques

Clear and supportive communication is key to working with actors effectively:

- Foster trust and create a comfortable on-set environment
- Emphasize character objectives and motivations over prescribing emotions
- Use action verbs to provide clear, actionable direction
- Offer context and backstory to deepen actors' understanding of their roles

Why it's important: Strong communication helps actors deliver authentic and emotionally resonant performances.

Pulling the Best Performance

To draw out compelling performances from actors:

- Encourage improvisation and collaboration to explore character depth
- Provide physical tasks or props to help actors stay engaged
- Promote active listening and genuine reactions between actors

Why it matters: These techniques contribute to believable performances that connect with audiences on an emotional level.

Working with the Director of Photography

A successful collaboration between the director and cinematographer ensures a strong visual narrative by:

- Clearly communicating the visual vision using references or storyboards
- Discussing camera placement, movement, and framing to support the story

- Aligning on a cohesive visual style that enhances the film's themes and tone

Why it's essential: This partnership ensures that all visual elements work harmoniously to tell a compelling story.

On-Set Problem-Solving

Directors must be adept at handling unforeseen challenges by:

- Staying adaptable and open to creative solutions when facing limitations
- Maintaining a calm and composed demeanor to keep the team focused
- Prioritizing problem-solving strategies that serve the story best

Why it's critical: Strong leadership and quick thinking keep the production on track and foster a positive, solution-oriented atmosphere.

By mastering these key aspects of directing, filmmakers can bring their unique vision to life, crafting impactful films that resonate with audiences on a deeper level.

Chapter 4:

Shotlisting - A Crucial Tool for Filmmakers

Shotlisting is a vital step in filmmaking that involves creating a detailed document outlining every shot needed for a film or video project. This planning tool plays a crucial role in enhancing the production process and ensuring a smooth workflow.

Why Shotlisting Matters

1. **Visual Storytelling**
   A shot list acts as a blueprint for visual storytelling, enabling filmmakers to carefully plan and visualize each shot. This ensures that the intended message and emotions are effectively conveyed to the audience.

2. **Efficiency**
   A well-prepared shot list streamlines the production process by providing a clear roadmap. It helps manage resources effectively, minimizing delays and optimizing time on set.

3. **Communication**
   Shot lists serve as a shared reference point for the entire crew, ensuring everyone understands the director's vision and the specific requirements for each scene.

4. **Problem-Solving**
   With a detailed shot list, directors can quickly adapt to unexpected challenges on set, ensuring essential shots are captured even if changes occur.

Creating an Effective Shot List

To develop a comprehensive shot list:

1. Break down the script scene by scene.
2. Use storyboards to visualize key moments.
3. List each shot, including details such as camera angles, movements, and framing.
4. Organize shots by shooting day, taking logistics like location and actor availability into account.

Elements to Include

A thorough shot list should contain:

- Scene and shot numbers

- Description of the action
- Camera angles and movements
- Shot size (e.g., wide, medium, close-up)
- Key props or set elements
- Actors involved
- Any special equipment needed

Benefits of Shotlisting

1. **Enhancing Creativity**
   Planning shots in advance allows filmmakers to explore creative options and experiment with different visual approaches.

2. **Budget Management**
   A detailed shot list aids in efficient resource allocation, potentially reducing costs.

3. **Quality Control**
   Ensures all necessary shots are captured, maintaining the intended visual style and narrative flow.

While a shot list is an invaluable planning tool, maintaining flexibility on set is equally important. The ability to adapt to unexpected circumstances while staying true to the overall vision is a hallmark of a successful filmmaker.

Chapter 5:

Production - Turning Plans into Reality

Running an Efficient Set

Running a smooth film production set demands meticulous planning and seamless coordination across various departments. Success hinges on establishing clear communication channels and structured workflows to enhance productivity. Key elements of an efficient set include:

- Distributing a detailed shooting schedule and call sheet to all crew members.
- Ensuring all equipment and resources are prepared and in place before filming begins.
- Maintaining open communication between the director, assistant directors, and department heads.
- Adhering to safety protocols and industry best practices.
- Keeping the set organized and free from unnecessary clutter or distractions.

Key Departments and Their Functions

A successful production relies on the collaboration of several core departments, each with specialized roles and responsibilities:

- **Production Department:** Manages logistics, scheduling, budgeting, and overall project coordination.
- **Camera Department:** Oversees the visual capture of the film, including camera operation, lighting, and composition.
- **Sound Department:** Ensures high-quality audio recording, covering dialogue, ambient sound, and on-set audio needs.
- **Art Department:** Develops the visual style through set design, props, and costumes to align with the film's vision.
- **Makeup and Hair Department:** Ensures actors' appearances align with their characters and maintains continuity throughout the shoot.
- **Grip and Electric Department:** Handles lighting setups, power distribution, and camera support systems.

Maintaining a Productive Atmosphere

Creating a productive atmosphere on set is essential to keep morale high and operations running smoothly. Effective strategies include:

- Encouraging a positive and respectful work environment.
- Providing clear direction and expectations to the crew.
- Recognizing and appreciating good work.
- Addressing conflicts or issues promptly and professionally.
- Allowing for proper breaks and meal times to sustain energy levels.
- Minimizing distractions and maintaining focus during filming.

Shooting for the Edit

Smart production practices consider how footage will be assembled during post-production. Key principles for shooting with editing in mind include:

- Capturing ample coverage of each scene, including master shots, close-ups, and cutaways.
- Ensuring continuity in action, lighting, and performance across multiple takes.

- Avoiding drastic shifts in shot sizes to maintain visual coherence.
- Recording room tone and wild lines for seamless sound design in post-production.
- Properly slating each take to streamline the organization of footage during editing.

Handling Unforeseen Challenges

Even with thorough preparation, unexpected challenges can arise on set. Approaches to effectively manage these include:

- Staying adaptable and flexible in response to changing circumstances.
- Developing contingency plans for common issues such as weather disruptions or equipment malfunctions.
- Prioritizing essential shots and making informed decisions about necessary adjustments.
- Tapping into the expertise of experienced crew members to devise creative solutions.
- Keeping open communication with producers and stakeholders regarding significant changes or delays.

By focusing on these essential areas, production teams can successfully transform their plans into reality, ensuring the creation of a compelling and polished film or video project.

Chapter 6:

Post-Production - Piecing It All Together

Post-production is the final and critical phase of filmmaking where all the creative elements merge to produce the finished piece. This stage encompasses editing, sound design, visual effects, color grading, and preparing the film for distribution.

The Editing Process

Editing is the craft of shaping raw footage into a cohesive narrative. It involves selecting the best takes, structuring scenes, and establishing a rhythm that captivates the audience.

Key stages in the editing process:

1. **Logging Footage:** Organizing and labeling raw clips for easy access.
2. **Assembly Cut:** Constructing an initial version of the film with all potential footage.
3. **Rough Cut:** Refining the assembly cut to focus on story structure and pacing.
4. **Fine Cut:** Further polishing the edit, concentrating on precise cuts and transitions.

5. **Final Cut:** The approved version, ready for sound and visual enhancements.

Collaborating with an Editor

A successful collaboration between the director and editor is essential to realizing the film's vision. Here are some tips for effective teamwork:

- Provide a clear vision and goals for the film.
- Allow creative freedom while maintaining open dialogue.
- Be receptive to new ideas and constructive feedback.
- Maintain consistent communication throughout the process.

Sound Design and Foley Art

Sound design enhances the film's atmosphere and storytelling by crafting audio elements that complement the visuals. Foley, named after sound effects pioneer Jack Foley, recreates everyday sounds to enhance realism.

Essential elements of sound design and Foley:

- **Dialogue Editing:** Cleaning and enhancing spoken content.

- **Sound Effects:** Creating or sourcing sounds that support the narrative.
- **Foley Recording:** Adding sounds like footsteps, clothing rustles, and object interactions.

Color Grading and Visual Effects

Color grading adjusts and enhances the footage's color to achieve a specific look, while visual effects (VFX) add or alter imagery beyond what was captured on set.

Color grading workflow:

1. Shoot in RAW or LOG format for maximum flexibility.
2. Apply color correction to balance and normalize the footage.
3. Perform primary grading to set the overall tone.
4. Utilize secondary grading for targeted adjustments.

VFX work is typically completed before final color grading to ensure seamless integration.

Music Scoring and Licensing

Music significantly influences the emotional impact

of a film. Filmmakers can opt for original scores or licensed tracks to enhance the storytelling.

Key music licensing considerations:

- Secure proper sync and master use licenses for existing music.
- Work with Performance Rights Organizations (PROs) such as ASCAP, BMI, or SESAC.
- Determine licensing fees based on the film's budget and distribution strategy.

For original scores, composers often work on a "work-for-hire" basis, assigning rights to the production company.

Preparing Deliverables for Distribution

Deliverables are the final assets required for releasing and marketing the film. These typically include:

1. Digital Formats:

- ProRes or Digital Cinema Package (DCP)
- Audio files (5.1 surround mix, music & effects tracks, dialogue stems)

2. **Legal Documentation:**

    - Chain of title documentation
    - Errors and Omissions (E&O) insurance
    - Music licenses and cue sheets

3. **Marketing Assets:**

    - High-resolution stills
    - Poster artwork
    - Trailers
    - Press kits (including synopsis, production notes, and cast/crew bios)

Proper preparation of deliverables ensures a smooth distribution process and enhances the film's chances for success.

Post-production is where a filmmaker's vision truly takes shape. Mastering each component of this stage allows for the creation of compelling, polished projects ready to captivate audiences.

Chapter 7:

Chain of Title - Own it

Chain of title documents are a fundamental component of the filmmaking process, serving as the legal foundation that confirms ownership and rights to every aspect of a film production. These documents establish a clear record that ensures the production company has secured all necessary rights to produce, distribute, and profit from the film.

Key Components of Chain of Title Documents

Script-Related Documents

1. **Copyright Registration** - Official registration with the U.S. Copyright Office to protect the script.
2. **Certificate of Authorship** - A signed declaration from the script's author(s) affirming the originality of the work.
3. **Screenplay Assignment Agreement** - A document transferring screenplay rights from the writer to the production company.
4. **Option Agreement** - Grants the production company exclusive rights to

purchase a script based on pre-existing material within a set timeframe.
5. **Purchase Agreement** - Finalizes the transfer of rights from the original copyright holder to the production company.

Underlying Rights Documents

1. **Life Story Rights Agreement** - Necessary when a film is based on a real person's life.
2. **Book Adaptation Agreement** - Required for adapting content from a published book.
3. **Trademark Clearances** - Documentation confirming permission to use trademarked elements in the film.

Production-Related Documents

1. **Talent Release Forms** - Agreements from actors authorizing the use of their performances.
2. **Crew Release Forms** - Similar agreements for crew members.
3. **Location Release Forms** - Permissions to film at specific locations.
4. **Music Licensing Agreements** - Contracts for original compositions and licensed tracks.

5. **Copyright Clearances** - Authorizations for the use of copyrighted logos, costumes, product placements, and more.

Post-Production Documents

1. **Post-Production Release Agreements** - Contracts with editors, visual effects artists, and post-production teams.
2. **Distribution Agreements** - Contracts outlining terms with distributors for various territories or platforms.
3. **Errors and Omissions (E&O) Insurance Policy** - Proof of insurance to mitigate legal risks.

The Importance of a Clean Chain of Title

Maintaining a clear chain of title is critical for several reasons:

1. **Legal Protection** - Shields the production from potential copyright disputes.
2. **Facilitating Distribution** - Distributors require proof of ownership before agreeing to release the film.
3. **Securing Financing** - Investors often demand evidence of a clean chain of title before funding a project.

4. **Insurance Requirements** - E&O insurers typically mandate a clean chain of title.
5. **International Co-Productions** - Many international partnerships require documented proof of ownership for official recognition.

Best Practices for Managing Chain of Title

1. **Start Early** - Begin assembling documentation from the project's inception.
2. **Chronological Organization** - Arrange documents in chronological order for easy verification.
3. **Regular Updates** - Continuously update the chain of title as new documents are created.
4. **Professional Review** - Consult with an entertainment lawyer to verify the completeness and validity of documents.
5. **Copyright Registration** - While not mandatory, registering copyright transfers can reinforce the chain of title.

By diligently maintaining a well-organized chain of title, filmmakers can safeguard their creative and financial investments. This meticulous approach ensures a smoother journey from development to distribution, preventing legal hurdles and securing the film's path to its intended audience.

Chapter 8:

Distribution and Marketing Strategies

Identifying Your Audience

Understanding your target audience is fundamental to successful film distribution and marketing. To effectively identify your audience:

- Analyze your existing customer base through surveys and interviews to gain insights into their preferences and behaviors.
- Conduct market research to stay informed about industry trends and audience demands.
- Develop detailed audience personas considering demographics (age, gender, income) and psychographics (interests, values, lifestyle).
- Utilize demographic segmentation as a starting point, but go deeper to understand what drives your audience.
- Acknowledge that multiple audience segments may exist, and tailor your strategies to address their unique needs.

Research suggests that focusing on three key audience groups is a commonly effective approach.

The Festival Circuit

Film festivals serve as a powerful tool for distribution and marketing:

- Carefully select festivals that align with your film's genre and intended audience.
- Leverage festivals as opportunities to network, gain exposure, and potentially secure distribution deals.
- Prepare comprehensive marketing materials, such as postcards, posters, and an engaging social media presence.
- Engage with local media through interviews to generate buzz and attract attention.
- Gather audience feedback and encourage reviews on platforms like Letterboxd and IMDb to build credibility and visibility.

Design your festival strategy around specific goals, whether they include winning awards, networking, or building a dedicated audience base.

Online Platforms and Streaming Services

Digital distribution continues to reshape the film industry landscape. Key platforms to consider include:

- Major platforms like YouTube, Vimeo, and Amazon Prime Video.
- Niche platforms tailored to specific genres or audiences, such as IndieFlix or MUBI.
- Regional platforms catering to local markets, like JioCinema in India or Showmax in Africa.

Evaluate each platform based on audience reach, revenue potential, and available features to determine the best fit for your film. Distribution services like FilmHub or Quiver can help streamline the process while allowing you to maintain control over your rights and royalties.

Traditional vs. Self-Distribution

Each distribution approach comes with its own set of advantages and challenges:

Traditional Distribution:

- Provides access to established networks and marketing resources.
- Handles logistics and negotiations with exhibitors.
- Involves sharing a portion of the profits, typically 20-30%.

Self-Distribution:

- Grants greater control over marketing and release strategies.
- Offers potential for higher profits if executed effectively.
- Requires significant time, effort, and upfront investment.
- May limit reach without established industry connections.

When deciding between these options, consider your film's budget, target audience, and available resources.

Crafting a Marketing Strategy

An effective marketing strategy should encompass:

- Clear objectives and key performance indicators (KPIs) to measure success.
- A balanced mix of traditional and digital marketing tactics.
- Content marketing through blogs, behind-the-scenes videos, and social media storytelling.
- Paid advertising on platforms where your audience is most active.
- Public relations efforts to generate media coverage and industry buzz.

- Creation of compelling assets such as trailers, posters, and press kits.

Tailor your strategy to align with your audience and financial constraints, remaining flexible to adapt based on performance insights.

The Importance of Networking

Networking plays a critical role in the film industry:

- Attend industry events, festivals, and workshops to establish valuable connections.
- Engage with industry professionals on social media platforms like LinkedIn and Twitter.
- Become a member of professional organizations and online communities to expand your network.
- Focus on building authentic relationships by offering value and support to others.
- Maintain long-term connections through consistent follow-up and engagement.

Effective networking is not just about collecting contacts but about fostering meaningful relationships that can lead to future collaborations, job opportunities, and industry insights.

By concentrating on these key elements—audience identification, festival planning, digital distribution, strategic marketing, and networking—filmmakers can enhance their chances of success in the competitive realm of film distribution and marketing.

Chapter 9:

Understanding Your Target Audience

Research Your Genre and Subgenres

To effectively connect with your audience, start by exploring your film's genre and subgenres. This deep dive will help you grasp:

- The typical characteristics and storytelling conventions within your genre
- The existing fan base and current market trends
- Insights from successful films with similar themes

Leverage resources such as online databases, industry publications, blogs, and film forums to gather valuable information.

Analyze Competitors

Studying films within your genre, particularly recent releases and upcoming projects, provides crucial insights. Through competitor analysis, you can identify:

- Strengths and potential gaps within your film
- Market opportunities and possible challenges
- Effective marketing strategies and distribution channels

Platforms like IMDb, Box Office Mojo, and Rotten Tomatoes offer performance metrics that can guide your strategy.

Define Audience Demographics

Pinpointing the fundamental characteristics of your target audience is key. Consider factors such as:

- Age
- Gender
- Income level
- Education background
- Geographic location
- Cultural background

Gather this data through surveys, interviews, focus groups, and analytics tools to ensure accuracy.

Develop Audience Personas

Craft detailed profiles of your ideal viewers based

on real-world data. These audience personas should include:

- Demographic details
- Interests, values, and motivations
- Viewing habits and preferences

Personas serve as a guide to shape creative decisions and marketing efforts, helping you resonate with specific audience segments.

Conduct Market Research

Use various research methods to gain valuable insights into your film concept, messaging, and themes. Effective approaches include:

- Direct interviews with potential viewers
- Observational studies
- Social media trend analysis
- Focus groups and online surveys

This research helps refine your film's appeal and align it with audience expectations.

Test Your Assumptions

Creating a minimum viable product (MVP),

such as a teaser or short preview, allows you to validate audience interest. Share this content with a selected group of viewers to gather feedback and fine-tune your approach.

Explore Psychographics

Going beyond basic demographics, understanding your audience's psychographic profile provides deeper insights. Focus on factors like:

- Lifestyle choices
- Hobbies and interests
- Core values and beliefs
- Attitudes toward media consumption

This knowledge helps create a more meaningful connection with your audience.

Analyze Media Consumption Habits

Understanding where and how your audience consumes content is crucial. Different age groups engage with media in unique ways, which should influence your distribution and promotional strategies. Identify preferred platforms such as:

- Streaming services
- Social media channels
- Traditional media outlets

By applying these strategies, you can build a thorough understanding of your audience, ensuring your film reaches and resonates with the right viewers effectively.

Chapter 10:

Attracting Investors and Financing Your Film

Developing a Compelling Pitch

Crafting a compelling pitch is crucial for attracting investors to your film project. Your pitch should be concise, engaging, and highlight the unique aspects of your film. Key elements to include:

- **Logline:** A powerful one-sentence summary that captures the essence of your story.
- **Synopsis:** A brief overview of the plot, highlighting key characters and conflicts.
- **Unique Selling Points:** What makes your film stand out from others in the genre.
- **Target Audience:** Clearly define who your film is for and why it will resonate with them.
- **Key Team Members:** Highlight the experience and achievements of your director, producers, and any attached talent.
- **Visual Elements:** Use concept art, mood boards, or a teaser trailer to give investors a sense of your film's style and tone.

When delivering your pitch, remember to:

- Keep it brief, ideally under two minutes.
- Focus on compelling "hooks" that capture attention quickly.
- Tailor your pitch to each specific investor.
- Practice your delivery to ensure confidence and clarity.

Creating a Business Plan for Your Film

A comprehensive business plan is essential for demonstrating the financial viability of your project to potential investors. Your film business plan should include:

- **Executive Summary:** An overview of your project, emphasizing its unique selling points and potential for success.
- **Project Overview:** Details about the film's concept, genre, and target audience.
- **Market Analysis:** Insights on similar films' performance and your film's market potential.
- **Production Plan:** A timeline with key milestones and production strategy.

- **Marketing and Distribution Strategy:** A detailed plan for promoting and distributing your film.
- **Financial Projections:** Budget breakdowns, potential revenue streams, and return on investment projections.
- **Risk Assessment:** Identification of potential challenges and strategies to mitigate them.

Ensure your business plan is professional, well-researched, and tailored to your specific project. Use clear, concise language and include visual aids where appropriate to enhance understanding.

Finding and Approaching Investors

Identifying and approaching potential investors requires strategy and persistence. Effective methods include:

- **Networking:** Attend film festivals, industry events, and networking functions to meet potential investors.
- **Leveraging Personal Connections:** Reach out to friends, family, and colleagues who may be interested in investing.

- **Researching Potential Investors:** Seek individuals or firms with a history of investing in similar films.
- **Utilizing Online Platforms:** Use platforms like AngelList or LinkedIn to connect with potential investors.
- **Approaching Private Equity Firms:** Some firms specialize in film investments and may be interested in your project.

When approaching investors:

- Be professional and prepared with your pitch and business plan.
- Clearly explain the investment opportunity and potential returns.
- Be transparent about risks and challenges.
- Follow up promptly and maintain strong communication.

Crowdfunding Strategies

Crowdfunding can effectively raise funds while building an audience for your film. Successful strategies include:

- **Choosing the Right Platform:** Select a platform like Kickstarter, Indiegogo, or Seed&Spark that fits your project.
- **Setting a Realistic Goal:** Determine a funding target that covers your needs but is achievable within the campaign timeframe.
- **Creating Compelling Content:** Develop an engaging campaign page with a strong video pitch, compelling visuals, and a clear project description.
- **Offering Attractive Rewards:** Design enticing perks for different contribution levels.
- **Building a Strong Team:** Assemble a dedicated team to manage the campaign and engage with supporters.
- **Leveraging Social Media:** Use social networks to promote your campaign and update supporters regularly.
- **Engaging Your Audience:** Respond promptly to questions and comments, keeping backers involved in the filmmaking process.

Government Grants and Tax Incentives

Governments offer financial support for filmmaking through grants and tax incentives, which can significantly reduce production costs.

- **Research Available Grants:** Explore funding opportunities from national, state, and local film commissions.
- **Understand Eligibility Requirements:** Review criteria for grant and incentive programs to ensure your project qualifies.
- **Prepare Strong Applications:** Develop compelling grant proposals that align with funding objectives.
- **Explore Tax Incentives:** Many regions offer tax credits or rebates for film production; research locations that provide the best benefits.
- **Consider Co-Production Opportunities:** Some countries have co-production treaties that unlock additional funding.
- **Seek Professional Advice:** Consult with a film finance expert or entertainment lawyer for guidance.

Pitch Deck

A well-crafted pitch deck is a visual presentation that complements your verbal pitch and business plan. Key elements to include:

- **Title Slide:** Your film's title, tagline, and a compelling image that captures the essence of your project.
- **Logline and Synopsis:** A brief, engaging summary of your story.
- **Visual Style:** Mood boards or concept art to convey the film's aesthetic.
- **Character Profiles:** Introduce key characters with brief descriptions and potential casting ideas.
- **Market Analysis:** Data on your target audience and comparable films' performance.
- **Team Bios:** Highlight the experience and achievements of key crew members.
- **Budget and Timeline:** Overview of your production budget and schedule.
- **Marketing and Distribution Plan:** Your strategy for promoting and distributing the film.
- **Investment Opportunity:** Explanation of the investment structure and potential returns.

When designing your pitch deck:

- Keep it visually appealing and consistent with your film's style.
- Use high-quality images and graphics.
- Limit text and use bullet points for clarity.
- Ensure the deck flows logically and tells a compelling story.

By addressing these aspects of film financing, you'll be well-prepared to attract investors and secure the funding needed to bring your vision to life. Persistence, professionalism, and preparation are key throughout this journey.

Resources

Professional Script Format Templates

Using the right format is crucial when writing a screenplay to ensure readability and industry compliance. Here are some essential formatting guidelines:

- Use a 12-point Courier font.
- Set margins to 1.5 inches on the left and 1 inch on the top, bottom, and right.
- Begin each scene with a scene heading (slugline) in ALL CAPS.
- Introduce character names in ALL CAPS the first time they appear.
- Center character names above dialogue.
- Use parentheticals sparingly for brief actions or directions.
- Right-align transitions such as CUT TO:.

Recommended free script templates:

- **Final Draft Templates** - Industry-standard software with pre-formatted templates.
- **Google Docs** - Use proper formatting from examples above.

- **WriterDuet** - Free online screenwriting software with built-in formatting.
- **Celtx** - Free screenwriting software with various templates.

Tip: Customize the title page with your script's title, your name, and contact information.

Budgeting Spreadsheet Templates

A well-structured budget is essential for film production. Key components to include:

- **Above-the-line costs** (talent, writers, producers, director)
- **Below-the-line costs** (crew, equipment, locations, etc.)
- **Post-production costs**
- **Contingency funds** (typically 10-20% of the total budget)

Recommended free film budget templates:

- **StudioBinder Film Budget Template** - Auto-calculates expenses and grand total.
- **Google Sheets** - Use templates from examples above.

- **Wrapbook Film Budget Template** - Customizable Excel template.
- **Celtx Budget Template** - Included in Celtx's production management suite.

Tips for using a budget template:

- Tailor categories to suit your project needs.
- Use formulas to calculate totals automatically.
- Include notes for any unique expenses.
- Update regularly during pre-production.

Production Schedule Template

A production schedule helps organize daily shoot plans. Key elements to include:

- Scene numbers
- Locations
- Cast required
- Estimated setup and shooting times
- Equipment needs
- Special requirements (stunts, effects, etc.)

Recommended free production schedule templates:

- **StudioBinder Production Calendar** - Interactive online scheduling tool.
- **StudioBinder Stripboard Template** - Classic stripboard format in Google Sheets.
- **SetHero Production Schedule Template** - Customizable Excel template.

Tips for using a production schedule template:

- Use color-coding for different locations.
- Account for prep and wrap times.
- Schedule meal breaks and location moves.
- Update daily to reflect progress.

Call Sheet Template

A call sheet provides crucial daily details for the cast and crew. Key elements to include:

- Date and shoot day number
- General call time and location
- Individual call times for cast/crew
- Scenes being shot that day
- Weather forecast
- Important contact numbers

- Safety notes

Recommended free call sheet templates:

- **StudioBinder Call Sheet Template** - Customizable online template.
- **SetHero Call Sheet Template** - Professional Excel template.
- **Wrapbook Call Sheet Template** - Simple, printable PDF template.

Tips for creating call sheets:

- Verify all contact details.
- Provide clear parking and location instructions.
- Note any schedule changes from the previous day.
- Distribute the night before.

Shot List Template

A shot list details the specific shots needed for each scene. Key elements to include:

- Scene number
- Shot number
- Shot size (wide, medium, close-up, etc.)

- Camera movement (pan, tilt, dolly, etc.)
- Brief description of action
- Estimated time per shot

Recommended free shot list templates:

- **StudioBinder Shot List Template** - Customizable online template.
- **Boords Shot List Template** - Simple Google Sheets template.
- **Celtx Shot List** - Part of Celtx's pre-production tools.

Tips for using a shot list template:

- Include storyboard sketches if available.
- Identify special equipment needs (Steadicam, drone, etc.).
- Prioritize shots in case of time constraints.
- Review with the director and DP before shooting.

By using these professional templates, you can optimize your pre-production workflow and ensure all necessary documentation is in place for a seamless production process. Remember to personalize each template to align with your project's specific requirements.

Overcoming Challenges and Staying Inspired

Dealing with Creative Blocks

Creative blocks can be tough, but they're a natural part of the creative journey. Here are some effective ways to push through them:

1. **Switch up your environment.** A change of scenery—whether it's a walk in the park, visiting an art exhibit, or working in a different space—can stimulate new ideas.

2. **Experiment with new techniques.** Trying an unfamiliar medium or approach can spark fresh inspiration and reignite your creativity.

3. **Break projects into smaller tasks.** Setting achievable goals helps you build momentum and avoid feeling overwhelmed.

4. **Reflect on past successes.** Keeping a collection of your best work can remind you of your capabilities and fuel your confidence.

5. **Take intentional breaks.** Engaging in activities you love—like reading, listening to music, or spending time in nature—can refresh your mind and spark new ideas.

Inspiring Example: J.K. Rowling, the author of the Harry Potter series, faced countless rejections before achieving success. Despite creative and financial challenges, she persevered, ultimately crafting one of the most beloved book series of all time.

Managing Stress on Set

The fast-paced nature of production work can be overwhelming. Here are some strategies to keep stress in check:

1. **Practice deep breathing and short relaxation techniques.** Even a few moments of mindfulness can help you stay centered.

2. **Stay present.** Focusing on your immediate task can help eliminate distractions and

reduce feelings of pressure.

3. **Put things in perspective.** Most challenges on set are temporary and solvable.

4. **Prioritize your tasks.** Good time management and learning to say no to unnecessary commitments can ease workload pressure.

5. **Make self-care a priority.** Regular breaks and downtime help prevent burnout and keep you energized.

Inspiring Example: Christopher Nolan faced enormous pressure while directing "Inception," a complex and ambitious film. By maintaining focus and taking things one step at a time, he successfully brought his vision to life.

Learning from Failure

Failure is an essential part of growth. Here's how to turn setbacks into stepping stones:

1. **See failure as a lesson.** Every misstep brings insights that can lead to future success.

2. **Evaluate and adjust.** Identify what went wrong and use it as a guide for improvement.

3. **Adopt a growth mindset.** Embrace challenges as opportunities to refine your skills and grow stronger.

4. **Seek feedback.** Talking to others about your failures can provide new perspectives and actionable solutions.

5. **Use setbacks as motivation.** Let failures push you to work harder and smarter.

Inspiring Example: Thomas Edison once said, "I have not failed. I've just found 10,000 ways that won't work." His relentless experimentation ultimately led to groundbreaking inventions like the light bulb.

Staying Passionate About Your Craft

Long-term success requires sustained passion and motivation. Here's how to keep the fire alive:

1. **Keep learning.** Attend workshops, watch tutorials, and stay up-to-date with industry trends.

2. **Collaborate with others.** Working with fellow creatives can offer fresh perspectives and new inspiration.

3. **Pursue passion projects.** Set personal goals outside of client work to freely explore your creativity.

4. **Reconnect with your why.** Reflect on what initially drew you to your craft and let that drive you forward.

5. **Celebrate your progress.** Acknowledging milestones, no matter how small, keeps you motivated and inspired.

Inspiring Example: Walt Disney faced numerous setbacks, including bankruptcy and losing the rights to one of his first successful characters.

However, his unwavering passion for storytelling led him to create Mickey Mouse and build a global entertainment empire.

By embracing these strategies and drawing inspiration from those who have overcome similar challenges, you can navigate the ups and downs of the creative process, stay motivated, and continue evolving in your craft.

Epilogue

Your Next Steps in Filmmaking

Embarking on your filmmaking journey is an exciting and continuous learning experience. Here are key steps to help you grow and refine your craft:

1. Practice Consistently

The best way to improve as a filmmaker is to create. Theory is valuable, but nothing replaces hands-on experience. Start working on short films, documentaries, or passion projects. Every project you complete will provide insights and lessons that can't be found in books or tutorials alone.

2. Collaborate and Network

Filmmaking thrives on collaboration. Seek opportunities to connect with other creatives—whether it's through local film groups, festivals, or professional sets. Building relationships within the industry opens doors to new opportunities and invaluable mentorship.

3. Find Your Unique Voice

As you gain experience, focus on developing your

own artistic vision and storytelling style. Experiment with different genres and techniques to discover what truly resonates with you. Your distinct perspective is what will set your work apart and make it memorable.

Recommended Resources to Expand Your Knowledge

To deepen your understanding of filmmaking, consider exploring the following books and learning platforms:

Essential Filmmaking Books

- *The Filmmaker's Handbook* by Steven Ascher and Edward Pincus – A comprehensive resource covering all aspects of film production.
- *On Directing Film* by David Mamet – Practical insights into the director's craft from an industry veteran.
- *In the Blink of an Eye* by Walter Murch – A must-read on the art of film editing and storytelling.
- *Making Movies* by Sidney Lumet – A masterful exploration of the filmmaking process from a director's perspective.

Online Learning Platforms

- **Filmmaker IQ** – Provides in-depth video essays on a wide range of filmmaking topics.
- **MasterClass** – Offers courses taught by legendary directors such as Martin Scorsese and Spike Lee.
- **Sundance Co//ab** – Features workshops and masterclasses led by industry professionals.

Formal Education Options

While not a requirement, attending film school can provide structured learning and valuable networking opportunities. Consider institutions like NYU, USC, or local community colleges if pursuing a degree aligns with your goals.

Final Thoughts

Success in filmmaking comes from a blend of knowledge, practice, and perseverance. Stay curious, embrace every challenge, and most importantly—keep creating. With dedication and passion, your storytelling abilities will continue to evolve, and your voice as a filmmaker will shine through.

Acknowledgement

I want to take a moment to express my deepest gratitude to everyone who has supported me throughout this journey. Whether you've been a part of my creative process, offered words of encouragement, or simply believed in my vision, your support has meant the world to me.

To my family and friends—thank you for your unwavering belief in my dreams and for standing by me through every challenge and triumph. Your love, patience, and encouragement have been my foundation, and I am forever grateful for your presence in my life.

To my mentors and peers in the filmmaking industry—your insights, guidance, and shared experiences have been invaluable. Learning from you has shaped me into the filmmaker and entrepreneur I am today. I appreciate the time you've taken to share your wisdom and inspire my creative growth.

A heartfelt thank you to my incredible audience and readers—your enthusiasm and support fuel my passion. Whether you've followed my work, attended my workshops, or picked up this book, your trust and belief in my vision inspire me to keep pushing boundaries and telling meaningful stories.

Finally, to those who have challenged me along the way—thank you for pushing me to strive for excellence. Your feedback and perspectives have helped me grow and refine my craft.

This journey is far from over, and I am excited to continue creating, learning, and sharing with you all. Thank you for being a part of it. Your support makes all the difference, and I am truly grateful.

About The Author

Teddy Van Gough My name is Teddy Van Gough—a name that reflects both my teddy bear-like physique and my passion for creating artistic masterpieces.

So, what qualifies me to share my filmmaking knowledge in this book? Great question.

From an early age, I was captivated by the worlds of drawing and writing. Inspired by my cousin, Brandon, a masterful artist, I spent countless hours tracing his work, determined to develop my own creative style. Over time, storytelling became my true calling. In the 5th grade, my teacher, Mrs. Bailey, recognized my advanced English skills and encouraged me to explore poetry. This encouragement led me to win my first poetry contest in the 7th grade—igniting my journey as a writer.

Since then, I have authored a poetry book, a biopic, two stage plays, and four full-length feature screenplays. My directorial portfolio includes two feature films and an extensive catalog of short films. Additionally, I have produced award-winning projects such as Cupid's Christmas and Wake, collaborating with talented individuals like Fivel Stewart.

Beyond filmmaking, I excelled as a high school football and track star, earning All-State honors and playing in the 2005 Michigan High School All-Star Game at the University of Michigan. I pursued higher education in Business at Lane College in Jackson, TN, and Film at the Motion Picture Institute in Troy, MI. My commitment to continuous learning has led me to earn certifications as an Adobe Premiere Pro editor, a Meta-certified social media manager and marketer, a certified film trailer editor, and an FAA Part 107 licensed drone pilot, among others.

While my knowledge and experience continue to grow, I am dedicated to sharing my expertise with aspiring filmmakers. Through this eBook, my goal is to contribute to the future of filmmaking—empowering the next generation to craft compelling stories and potentially create the next groundbreaking film that shapes the world.

Screenwriter's Workbook:
Character Development Exercise

This exercise will help you create rich, multidimensional characters for your screenplay.

Step 1: Character Basics
Create a new character by filling in the following details:

- Name:_____
- Age:_____
- Occupation:_____
- Physical appearance:
- Hobbies:

Step 2: Character Background
Answer these questions about your character's past:

1. Where did they grow up?
   _____
   _____

2. What was their family life like?
   _____
   _____
   _____

3. What was a pivotal moment in their childhood?
   _____
   _____
   _____

4. What is their biggest regret?
   _____
   _____
   _____
   _____

Step 3: Character Motivations
Define your character's driving forces:

1. What is their immediate goal?
   _____
   _____
   _____

2. What is their long-term dream?

_____
_____
_____
_____

3. What obstacle stands in their way?

_____
_____
_____
_____

4. What is their biggest fear?

_____
_____
_____
_____

Step 4: Character Relationships
Describe two key relationships in your character's life:

1. A positive relationship (friend, mentor, lover):

_____
_____
_____
_____

2. A negative relationship (rival, enemy, disapproving family member):

Step 5: Character Voice
Write a short monologue (5-7 sentences) in your character's voice, revealing their personality and mindset.

_____
_____
_____
_____
_____
_____
_____
_____
_____
_____

Step 6: Character Arc
Outline a potential character arc:

1. Where does your character start emotionally / mentally?_____
_____
_____
_____
_____
_____
_____

2. What event could trigger a change?
_____
_____
_____
_____

3. How might they evolve by the end of the story?

Step 7: Integration
Consider how this character might fit into your current story idea or how they could inspire a new narrative. Write a brief scene (1-2 paragraphs) featuring this character in action.

Remember, the goal of this exercise is to create a well-rounded character with depth and complexity. Take your time with each step, and don't be afraid to revise and expand on your ideas as you go. This character development process can serve as a foundation for your screenplay, helping you craft authentic, engaging narratives.

THE DIRECTOR'S NOTEBOOK

Use this as a check list along the path of building your own Director's Notebook.

1. Play/Script Analysis

- Title and author:
  _____
  _____
  _____

- Synopsis:
  _____
  _____
  _____

- Themes and main ideas:
  _____
  _____
  _____

- Structure and plot analysis
  _____
  _____

_____
_____

- Key scenes and moments

_____
_____
_____

2. Research and Context
- ☐ Historical background
- ☐ Cultural significance
- ☐ Previous productions or adaptations
- ☐ Relevant social or political issues

3. Artistic Vision
- ☐ Overall concept
- ☐ Directorial approach
- ☐ Intended audience impact
- ☐ Visual style and aesthetic
- ☐ Shot list

4. Production Elements

Set Design
- ☐ Sketches or mood boards
- ☐ Layout and dimensions
- ☐ Materials and colors

Costume Design
- ☐ Character sketches
- ☐ Fabric swatches
- ☐ Color palette

Lighting Design
- ☐ Lighting plot
- ☐ Color schemes
- ☐ Special effects

Sound Design
- ☐ Music selections
- ☐ Sound effects list
- ☐ Audio cues

5. Blocking and Staging
- ☐ Stage diagrams
- ☐ Movement patterns
- ☐ Key positioning for important scenes

6. Character Development
- ☐ Character profiles
- ☐ Relationship maps
- ☐ Arc and growth throughout the story

7. Rehearsal Planning
- ☐ Schedule

- ☐ Warm-up exercises
- ☐ Scene breakdown
- ☐ Notes and adjustments

8. Technical Requirements
- ☐ Props list
- ☐ Special effects needs
- ☐ Audio-visual equipment

9. Inspiration and References
- ☐ Images
- ☐ Artwork
- ☐ Film or theater references

10. Production Timeline
- ☐ Pre-production tasks
- ☐ Rehearsal milestones
- ☐ Technical and dress rehearsals
- ☐ Opening night and run dates

This template provides a comprehensive framework for directors to organize their thoughts, plans, and creative vision. It can be easily customized to suit individual needs and preferences, allowing filmmakers to add or remove sections as necessary.

Notes:

Notes:

www.ingramcontent.com/pod-product-compliance
Lightning Source LLC
Chambersburg PA
CBHW070322100426
42743CB00011B/2519